Attitudes.........

Baby Steps........

BE.......

Beauty........

Blind Faith.........

Call.........

Choose Freedom.........

Dear Mom.........

Dream catching.........

Everyday.........

Evidence........

Fly ....

FreeLove.........

Gifts........

Give........

Golden........

Got it now.........

GreatLove..........

Grow..........

Hallelujah………

Hard work ………

Helped………

Help shine………

Hope held………

Humbled………

I can accept………

Inspiration……

Inspired………

Jesus is mine………

Love first………

Love is pt.1………

Love is pt.2……….

LoveGlue…….

Love is pt.3………

Meant it………

Men face men………

Motivation………

PeaceLove……….

Perfect aim………

Possible.........

Revelation..........

Shine...........

StarKid...........

Stay strong...........

SteadfastLove.........

Sure..........

Take off.........

Unique thoughts..........

Who understands.........

50. Wise.........

Attitudes reflect respect and leadership

Actions of an actor makes reality more sweeter

Appeasing self-esteem and egos

Each it's own is easier

Than trying to squeeze more peace from us

More faithful with a breather

So we're deep breathing, deep breaths

We keep steps and follow the code

Life is a beast pain is the season

Please don't swallow us whole

We need more heat from Love

The streets are gloves and sorrow is cold

They had a hold on us like today is great

But tomorrow is old

So oxymoronic and crossed-up

It's a toss-up for the reward

Let the past go. If you're fast, slow

Or you stand still just to see forward

Rather be bored than in chaos

Running out of doubts like a sea poured

Yes we want success and to release stress

Knowing patience is what we need more of

PSALM 17:4-5

With regard to the works of man, by the word of your lips I have avoided the ways of the violent. My steps have held fast to your paths; My feet have not slipped.

Baby steps

A long journey but it's worth it

Wasting weighs itself

The face of safety on the surface

Is it deep within?

Expected

Choose defeat or win

Courage

If you need a friend

Neglected

We can seek to end your hurting

Still baby steps

Slow motion and slow emergence

Live today yourself

Unless you feel faith is another person's

When you race in stealth

Be sure, mature, and capable

Sometimes, the need to stop and breathe

Is inescapable

I don't mean lazy steps

The past is passed

Tomorrow's distant

Just today is left

Just be consistent

Persevere

Pleasing is greatness felt

Beauty is a duty, its and action you should do it

Then you'll be it then we'll see it

We will love the way you prove it

Handsome is a ransom, can't earn it

But you can pay it

It's from gentlemen, no need for a leash

You will never have to say, "Sit!"

Beauty is what's ruling it's what's leading it's a teacher

Handsome is the answer to the question, it's a greeting

Blindness to what time is

When you only know what shine is

Soundless as a smile is but so loud

With Love behind it

Beauty is the future like computers yesterday

It is here, it is now it's the you that wasn't fake

It's the truth that wasn't cake

It's what's sweet but isn't ate

Being handsome is the He

It is the Me that wasn't late

So right on time, know what's at stake

Being fired or fired up!

It is beauty when you frown

And your Joy is inquired of

Being handsome is a Man's

An income that requires Love

Either beautiful is she or their eyes will never see

Be beautiful or handsome but also be at peace. How you act is who you are also. So Be more than we can see but be unable to he ignored.

BE

Beauty

Beauty to me is believing peace is perfect

Because if everything is peaceful

Keeping it sweet would be for certain

Beauty to me is deep

Not what we see just on the surface

And we're all beautiful people

Give us freedom we deserve it

Without the need to be nervous

We should be leaders we should be first

Who else to carry the blind

What's lost you find out if you search it

All in all is Love

It's the light God made the earth with

Equally beautiful features

Evenly measured

Nothing is worthless

Blind faith, but still strong

For real, long or short

Define great, reveal the face

Fulfill it's own remorse

Of course some lost, unfortunate cross

Transition back to the start

Am I in place, are you in place

What is panoramic art?

Blind faith, the time it takes

The effort applied to see

The rest of acquiring peace is learned

Ignore the desires to flee

In order to rise to relief

At first you decide to BE

A smile that is gone

But still so strong

Inspires

Revives your teeth

Blind faith, admire today

Just fire away, the target in place

A heart is displayed, you hear when it beats

It's clear and complete

No fear of deceit

Finally seen

No dream

I'm awake

I waited and made it a gift

Was blind in a way

But still I had faith

His Will got rid of the filth

PSALM 145:17-18

The LORD Is righteous in all his ways and kind in his works. The LORD is near to all who call on him, to all who call on him in truth.

A heartfelt promise believed in

So keep calling

Stay near and fear him

He's faithful to keep talking

His Instructions set to light the way

His glory you'll reach often

Before regrets can set

He'll bury deceit's coffin

How you love

Know who you live for

As God's child

Unique depiction of what's lit

That's IT!

Even in odd style

Jesus: Brother

Jesus: Friend

Jesus: Then and Now

Jesus covers, he is dependable

When in doubt

You can shout it or just whisper

If you let him

He comes nearer

You should love

He sees your love as He sees in a mirror

Choose Freedom

Locked up but no need for a shot cup

Stay sober minded

Build a structure, face the construction you make

Don't go behind it

Hey, be faithful over blindness

See again

Reality is freedom and we <u>choose</u> to be free again

Not in prisons of our conditions

Impress with the first expression

In prison but not imprisoned

Inspections the worst expected

Escaped from the hurts, neglected

Let pain fall away

Locks with no keys are the worst, a weapon

Insane, but all is safe

Labeled an inmate

A crook from crooked roads

We should have went straight

Temptation won the battle

Prison's bitterness could tempt hate

But friend wait!

Don't let the time do you

Be free and have a new view

It's time to be labeled too true

It seemed all of thoughts failed

And that hell was in a cell

And that peace could be achieved with

Just a few soups

Then I realized that true freedom is in the heart!

Dear Mom, when I needed you

Heaven you would appear from

Told me , don't get caught in greed

Taught me not to fear none

"Be clear son, get on your knees.

Thanks to the LORD that you can breathe."

To make Him proud I said out loud

That Jesus Christ is all I need

I know He can, now I'm a man

Remember when I wasn't though?

Remember when I'd cry at first

Then hide it so "weak" doesn't show

Now tears can flow I'm strong enough

I've grown in Love and pride died

Shame is lame, I gain from pain

Some things I cannot hide inside

My light is lit. How bright is it?

Your son I am, the night is fried

Like day always, "Be great always!"

I may. I might. I fail. I tried.

I'll try again, you taught me how to maintain

How if I could not stand the heat

Or if I can't hang

Then stay away from fire or get better legs

I appreciate the food I ate you kept us fed

I am thankful for the tools you gave

To step instead of giving up

Mom, you deserve the world

Even that would not be big enough

PROVERBS 23:25

Let your father and mother be glad and let her who gave you birth Rejoice.

Dream Catching

Catch it at it's highest peak

No hide and seek, you see it

Now reattached and can't deny it's sweet

Don't taste the flavor

Be it

Never wait, don't waste succeeding

Pro act and proceed to complete us

When it all seems sold be humble and bold

It'll get lonely, I know you need trust

And to be heated up

When it all seems cold

It's a lesson for those that lead us

A focus for drive, don't want to be drove

Just cautious before I speak up

When flawless, so perfect, I know that it's worth

My patience because we need love

To relieve us and to speed up

The reality of what you dream of

Everyday I awake with a smile

Thank God my eyes opened

All focus be reconciled

I am alive I applied hope in

One of the spokesmen for His gospel

The Father, Son, and Holy Ghost in

Faith, love, and forgiveness

The power of God will mold it

Yeah, trials and tribulations gone come

But don't leave you frozen

He won't give you too much to bare

To carry or load in

I know sins and I know friends

If you keep Jesus as your closest

You'll never have to worry about tomorrow

He'll take hold of it

And you know you'll win

'Cause you're not trying to compete

You're just trying to be sweet

Evidence

Actions speak louder than words

Pay attention, earn a "Thank You"

I was told to reach my goals

And there is nothing that I can't do

How to handle adversity is easy

If you really want to

Swallow your pride, be humble inside

Follow the truth, renewing your angle

Eye on the prize, motivated to rise

No reason to hide more evident proof

Designed for success, Let's will to be best

My scope is set, hopes the direction I shoot

In unity's house, now positive optimist

We should go do and leave doubts

No pessimist

If you need help with this

Brother I got you!

PSALM 55:6

And I say, "Oh, that I had wings like a dove! I would fly away and be at rest,

I won't complain but I wish to leave

I'm strong in pain

But I long and hope it gets relieved

The songs I sang

Can the lyrics help you fix the leak

I've grown, I came

So I hear, I'm here, you get to speak

Inform of Love

And the peace you hope you'll one day reach

Or have it now because you haven't drowned

Exist at ease

Let stress fade

Just let today be joyous made

It just may be your best day

When someone comes and says you're lazy

Just say that you test shade

They may understand

Because from stress,

They might hope resting in a Wonderland

Coconut palms, beaches, and sand

If I had wings I would fly from bad dreams

Don't want to land

Peace that's everlasting

If now was my only chance.....

PSALM 55:7

"yes, I would wonder far away,"

1 TIMOTHY 6:6-7

But Godliness with contentment is great gain, for we brought nothing into this world, and cannot take anything out of the world.

Standing up without doubt

About time

I'm giving all I can

A helping hand is in and outlined

Was born broke

But I hope your kids and house are fine

A storm came

Know storms come

Some storms train

And helps restore and reforms some

God is love, it's a charm gained

Content with who you share with

What you carry really gets heavy

But you can bare it

Strength isn't new to you

Your heart is not unusable

The only way to fall and to fail

Is you refuse to Do

But you did Do

That time when the world got critical

You kept a smile

That all the while was not invisible

Now take a deep breath....

Release

Peace

Give what you will

Love should be the first and last

Live what you feel

ROMANS 13:8

Owe no one anything, except to love each other, for then one who loves has fulfilled the law.

2 CORINTHIANS 9:7

Each one must give as he has decided in his heart, not reluctantly or under compulsion, for God loves a cheerful giver.

Gifts up, never give up

Never gave up, never will cut

Well and cheered up

Wheeled and steered right

At a red light but is geared up

Maybe downshift if the crown is lifted

Profound depiction, all around IF

We're in sound condition on a bound mission

To be high, flow away from the ground's filth

What words provoked

Who has heard it spoke

The the hope that you seek is in prayer's reach

You deserve the vote, be elected most

Most helpful to swept when you say what sweeps

Keep them off their feet with a footstool

You can look cool but can you see cool

Can you cheerfully give you handiwork?

And make the best out of working with each tool

There are three rules:

The first is: Love

The second: Live

The third is: Learning

Receive rewards for seeking the LORD

Your piece is the piece that His peace determines

2 CORINTHIANS 1:20

For all the promises of God find their yes in him. That is why it is through him that we utter our AMEN to God for his glory

2 CORINTHIANS 8.3

For they gave according to their means, as I can testify, and beyond their means, of their own accord.

Let's make the best out of what is given

Though in this moment we suffer, but have each other

A helper for your ambitions

Replace the mess under one condition

If it's for you

I'll keep cleaning, I'll go the distance

And working beyond it's meaning

I'm set to be under siege

No weapons ever defeats

The essence of pure compassion

Expressed when someone's complete

The whole way

Keep shining for a whole day

No one competes

2 CORINTHIANS 8:7

But as you excel in everything-in faith, in speech....

Just feel sweet

Give love free

Receive in return

You know that God is Love and you got His love

And it can be discerned

If you wonder what you have to give

If need be to learn...

2 CORINTHIANS 8:9

For you know the grace of our LORD Jesus Christ, that though he was rich, yet for your sake he became poor, so that you by his poverty might become rich.

I'm focused I see clear

I know where I'm going

We may not be responsible

For the words that are left unspoken

But to be heard by the herd, words have to be

Rounded-up and roped in

To chill will win some tickets

But verbs gone get some tokens

All the prizes won for rising

Now I feel alive I've been awoken

I never thought that sleep could be so deep

With needs unopened

Now I know that dreaming could be sweet

And keep us focused

If you're in tune and conscious

In control of your emotions

Then you're Golden

Got it Now

What do you see when you see me

It's gotta be fact 'cause I'm not fiction

Where would I be without this truth

Come running in last with lost position?

No contradiction, staying on track

I'll never go back without permission

Can I do this? Can I do that?

I do what I will with intuition

Feeling this feels like I am winning

From the beginning to the present

And from the present 'til I'm in heaven

God promised never to stop this blessing

Spiritual grace and relaxation

Considerate ways, so peace and patient

Do it for love and only for love

Erasing the envy, greed, and hating

We're all together, we should be better

Struggles should teach us elevation

Troubles, they come and go

We battle with focus

Life is a revelation

Moment to moment minute to minute

I think I was sent to set us straight

Narrowly made it but now you should know the way

Arrive for the celebration

EPHESIANS 5:6

Let no one deceive you with empty words.

Expecting a resurrection of faith; Revived

Let God make the connection

Just treasure to live today; Alive

Keep seeking first, His kingdom and righteousness

Be pure so you may abide

Your dreams of prosperity come to be

He won't say, "Denied!"

He's God, you won't say He lied

His word is a promise

He who's so worthy and honest

No weapon formed overcomes it

Don't be alarmed when the storm hits

Know peace and be still

He is the LORD, He keeps us

We know that we can just chill

Did you ask for the smile you have

Or praise for the way He made

He sent His only Son to die for you

So that you may be saved

Forgiven for your sin

He is risen so depend....

"Greater love has no one than this, that someone lay down His life for his friends."

JOHN 15:13

ROMANS 13:1-3

Let every soul be subject to the governing authorities that exist are appointed by God. Therefore whoever resists the authority resists the ordinance of God and those who resist will bring judgement on themselves. For rulers are not a terror to good works, but to evil. Do what is good, and you will have praise from the same.

Some will but not well

Reluctant to suck in their pride

Rebel but still don't prevail

Could chill and keep choosing to slide

Insistent on slickness

The crimeful mind sometimes helps to survive

Some fell but not well

Gone numb to protect what's inside

Double prison

Troubles persist, nothing but distance

Though we need freedom

Some only receives freedom's vision

So they fight against restraints that say they can't

They say the will though

Maybe it's greed or for speedy freedom

It's still slow

Not all who fall is fallen forever

You have to get it together

Not quite all problems get solved

But you replace peace for some pressure

Repeat resistance gets old

Believe to listen is better

You reach the peak of your bold

No need correcting a treasure

Emotion's commotion, feeling unload as a heart beat

Some focus, some lose control, some movements to:

Scarred feet

Or faith on an ocean

Walking on water for Love

I suppose if pressure makes diamonds

Faith creates stars up above

No doubts, no worries, just trust, be blessed

Be God's in a clutch

You can't be taken by Satan

Jesus rescues in a rush

He knows perfection and imperfection

Just know when to hush

And listen

If you can't bare it you'll get carried through afflictions

I denied myself to follow my LORD

So it's anonymous faith

I have a savior

His amazing grace has promised a way

Led into truth, given life

Love as an honest display

Bled to renew

Our gratitude is in our praise

Hard work on hard dirt

I think I may need more strength

To make a hole

To plant a seed

May you grow into long length

Stand tall dissolve greed

Sympathy

Not its own sense

To know you're there to know you care

Maybe who's wrong can be convinced

Have you felt like you could melt ice

With a bright smile

Or freeze cheese

Say cheese please

Camera flash! Nice style!

Someone is influenced when you're positive

Someone sees the key

That maybe you can teach them how to live

Regardless of how hard it is you keep working

Strenghth from what's consumed

Succeed with every seed

A rose you rise and bloom

JAMES 2:17

So also faith by it's self, if it does not have works is DEAD

Everybody needs a hand held

Helped up

Someone to shine in blind times

Who stepped up and took the lead

Committed to a fine line

You felt stuck?

But now you're free and able on a stable plane

You'll probably achieve the most

And all because you made a change

Not all about your self worth or self-esteem

Not that I'm less but, He's the Best! ---->

Sometimes, it's true, you may lose strength

Find peace because you needed rest

Perceive the test and recognize the virtues

Do what you can with rules

Punctuality at curfew

Go all the way, try hard not to reverse through

Or decline

The obstacles you face are not a waste

Soon all will be fine

In the mean time...Be ready with great faith

At the brink of, "Keep Succeeding!"

Initiate what should take place

PHILIPPIANS 4:13

I can do all tings through Him who strengthens me.

The first step is a step back

I can help, ask

If I can come

Though you've lost some

You can win some

Through experience earn your income

Where are friends from

From a help task

What's the meaning of a smile if you need one

Will you pay it back

Will you match the act

Or better yet, will you lead one

What's that smile for?

You already know

Just for yours I will give you mine first

Even simple things as a compliment

Those are mighty nice shoes and a fine shirt

And you wear it well

Do you care as well to seem us smile too

Then keep your smile on, it's contagious

And says there's a way to bliss

MATTHEW 5:14-16

"You are the light of the world. A city set on a hill cannot be hidden."Nor do people light a lamp and put it under a basket, but on a stand, and it gives light to all in the house." In the same way, let your light shine before men, that they may see your good works and glorify your father in heaven.

2 CORINTHIANS 5:7

For we live by faith, not by sight.

Hope held

Even though it seems that your scopes failed

Faith works

The Word of God enlivens

So we cope well

Believing to receive

Love we give and don't promote selves

A new path

A better place

This way instead of old trails

Stable stance

Enables chance, asserted for a purpose

In the wake of sands

The beach speaks with water on the surface

It depends though

How what's in is flowing or is out grown

Plenty seeds my pen is sowing

Reaping when the doubts are gone

Pride filled

Bound to what you're proud of

Sometimes it helps sometimes it hurts and makes shame

Seems like with ignorant egos it makes a cloud of

Something that's felt but then melts and turns to pain

The rain drops and can't stop the difficult fight

You know you're weak but still seeking the physical might

What you envision as right? If you position yourself?

With all humility's abilities conditioned to self

When you have love as your riches

Relationships as your wealth

When you've been covered:

Forgiveness

Have you forgiven yourself?

Do you determine books by the way they look?

Or do you read?

Does your pain consist of things you can't change

Or what you leave

Can you consider what you're missing

What is it that you received

Can you say prejudice has nothing to do with greed?

What do you register as truth

What you want? Or what is fact

You gotta forgive and give some love

And you gotta trust to get it back

Probably disgusted with the past and how you were hurt

But I bet the future is sweet in front of you

If you reverse

So it's not so bad to rearrange

Resettle yourself

Jesus is the name that you can call on

Forever for help

Since I did the same

My savior came and he never has left

Now I see plain

If it's all in vain I can accept

Inspiration

When it all just seems so right

And expressions come so easy

I might he blinded by this light

But I know it guides me if I need it

You are who I like, that is my reason

You may can help me find the way

Together, orchestrate perfection

Bae come help design Today

Inspiration? Motivation?

Focused straight, I think I see

I like this taste when I'm awake

So when we're sleep dreaming is sweet

Let's elevate and reach it's peak

Not rewind or reverse it

I'm ready for war of you're my rider

I'm tossing the first brick

No need to rehearse it

No practice with right now

I dive in it head first

With no thoughts that I might drown

It'll be worth it because I tried

That inspired light is found

This is special for someone special

Take care and wear it like a crown

Inspired by the "I" and "My"

The, "I am why, but you are too!"

The work I do but teamwork

Put others first if you are true

The, "Knew I grew"

A better Man

Not sure of views if words are few

But, "I" would do if a letter can

Forever stand

I need a plan

And a coward dies a thousands deaths

Incited some life, arouse some steps

I write is right and wrongful left

What's strong for self is strong for Us

What's gone is gone now new can come

Know many past has longed for trust

Put pride away

Receive some help

Do I deserve what Jesus did for me? I ask myself consistent. I can confess and accept His love, my actions must not contradict it. Mercy, peace, and love is what I pray for in the spirit. I know the sins that I committed yesterday has been forgiven. When I reflect on what he's brought me through or taught me from a distance, God's grace has brought me all this way. All the amazing grace I've witnessed. He's healed the sick the blind can see. He's released people from prison. My only request is if I can be the one that He sends fishing. Rejoice my friend, be sorrow free, Christ Jesus' love has risen. Holy spirit is strong when flesh is weak and sin is in remission. Love is patient, love is kind. Read chapter 13 of 1 CORINTHIANS. I realized, I need faith in his word. By faith it was written. Now hoping one day we'll receive white robes and no one is left behind. Praise and worshipping him in paradise with no concept of time. Eternal peace we yearn for, it's what we all need help to find. Jesus the Truth. Jesus the Light. Jesus the Way. Jesus is Mine!

GALATIANS 6:10

Therefore, as we have opportunity, let us do good to all people, especially to those who belong to the family of believers

Seek one

Reach one

Teach one

Do good to all

Each one

Feed them love

Contentment when the feast is done

Sleep some, rest well

Friendships should set sail

The wind blows with windows opened

Help to win

Then less fails

A blessed trail, prosperous paths

A chance to dance too

No I in team, not Me it's We

Just sharing to enhance YOU

Come in cool, the heat leaves

Delete greed in decent speed

Compassion could convince a fool

Have you planted recent seeds?

No odd advantage, even needs

Equal pieces= Peace

God commands to love abound

What does enough, what doesn't cease

Is love at least too much

Overwhelmed, but do not clutch

Release

You give it first, you'll feel it's worth

And treasure it as such a treat

Love Is...

Love is blind Love is divine

Love was designed to ease your stress

Love is work Love is a grind

Love is sometimes you need to rest

Love is trying, Love is a blessing

Love is complying, what's leading to best

Love is yours Love is mine

Love is not timed, no need for regrets

Love is a hug Love is a diamond

Love is the highest Love is above

Love is from God Love is from family

Love is a force, a push or a tug

Love is for free Love is for me

Love is for you and Love is a struggle

Love is a beast Love really hurts

We lose and afraid to give Love to another

Love I forgive Love I forget

Love I forgave Love is so crazy

Love is a meal Love I have ate

Love on a plate Love and some gravy

Love is the truth Love never lies

Love is confusing but never impatient

Love I can do so can I Love you?

True Love indeed is never complacent.

Love

Love is...How do you know what love is?

You're just a kid

I may not know just how and why

but teach me is what Love did

It taught me not to fault or blame

Just "Love is"

Not "Love was"

When misery hits I'm alive inside

Keep keeping me is what Love does

If you Love...Trust

If you Live...Laugh

If you Can...Smile

If you Will...Share

Because regardless of whatever pain came

You know Love heals and its still there

And you still care and it won't change

Because love is gain never Love lost

I could take a step just to help myself

But staying true to you is the Love's cost

Always give back never give up

Love is partly mine but it's more theirs

Life is hard but fair and with friendships...

I thinks the gathering is going to need more chairs

Because Love is there, who doesn't want some?

Oh, sure, yeah I'm young but I do know

When Love is

What Love is

And how to Show

1 JOHN 4:16

And we have known and believed the Love that God has for us. <u>God is Love,</u> and he who abides in love abides in God, and God in him.

COLOSSIANS 3:14

And above all these put on love, which binds everything together in perfect harmony

Love is glue if love is true

It helps to fix what's broken

Not love I say, by love I Do

Sometimes it isn't spoken

But still you know by my actions

The way, "I will" is in motion

Love to my wheel is the axle

I give, I'm turning it over

I give my time as a coach

So you can fly in first class

Maybe you'll fly into class first

Is there a <u>plane</u> way to ask?

Hey how are you?

How high are you?

Can I go too? If love is glue

Stay stuck to proof

We stick improved

Insistent bliss, exist as cool

Bound but free

Free but bound

Seek and found a use for ropes

Though the mountain peak was steep

Together, down

We ruled the slopes

Together up, Awoken hope

A better Us instead of broke

I know it's cold, though

Love can be your coat

COLOSSIANS 3:15

And let the peace of Christ rule in your hearts, to which indeed you were called in one body. And be thankful

THESSALONIANS 4:9

But concerning brotherly love you have no need that I should write to you, for you yourselves are taught by God to love one another.

Love is

Always knowing love is and love holds

Sometimes we question what it did

But sure that it's enough showed

Humanity is all people

Tall people

Small people

All equally set to receive relief from a rough road

Invest your strength and self-control

Then stress depletes as help unfolds

The one man's one hand can help someone else

Help is bold

Faith is courageous

Just saying hey is contagious

It just may brighten the day of someone

Who's day has been cold

Love is

Jesus taught me Love rose

No to say that love died

But with love applied, your trust grows

With trust you "get to" not you, "got to"

Love is with you

What can stop you?

God is Love

He keeps His grip and never drops you.

1 JOHN 4:11

Beloved, if God so loved us, we also ought to love one another

I meant everything I said

The verbs paint my picture clear

If you hurt I'll wipe that pain away

I promise not to miss a tear

I promise not to disappear

When some problems seem to squeeze

I'll bring peace and relaxation

Now everything can be at ease

All we need is a little faith

We can fly if you believe

All we have to do is pray

Then all you have to do is breathe

Deep breaths, never suffocate

Like life is just a breeze

Steep steps, but cool, it's all okay

'Cause ice was meant to freeze

Heat melts it, if we blaze

Burn it up, let's be the flame

Turn it up a few degrees

I learned to work for where I aim

You know who the target is

And you know you're the same

He who hit it should've earned a kiss

You know who to blame

Men face men

Face the challenge of time

Though I'm impatient, I'll make it

God has a balanced designed

Yet I still battle in mind

It's an emotional rollercoaster

We suffer, but Jesus is near

Our pain helps us hold Him closer

Lord, lead me

A Bolder Soldier

I kill with a kind heart

Quick death to the hate of

Brothers and sisters then shines start

Know once I was blind

Dark

Know now I can see and be seen

I once was the dirtiest first

Now filled up with glee to be clean

I'm driven by fear of the Lord

He gives me the gear of a King

A crown for His righteousness

And His word for a Sword

My faith is a Shied

I stand as clear as it seems

Thank God, my hope is restored

The evidence is revealed

JOHN 16:33

"I have said these things to you, that you may have peace. In the world you will have tribulation. But take heart, I have overcome the world."

Motivation

My reason for believing I can achieve it

I selected perfection to follow

How is peace proceeded

Tomorrow's goals of a leader

Written,

You read it

Be patient instead of greedy

Then maybe hollowness is filled with what you needed

Motivation's demonstration

Complacency not a factor

A portion of why we're working

Is garnished out of our character

Expression is what I speak of

Keep speaking in route to laughter

Keep us happy,

Storms

But joy is coming after

Inspiration is for free

So let's be it and liberated

For today is not the past

We got pass what we need to say

So let silence be your leader

More equal to even greatness

Motivation

No reason for a waiting list

Peace Love

How can I get a piece of

Or share my own

Hate could never conquer Love

With peace we always carry on

Be very strong not weak Love

I know you can so prove it

Not to viewers but to you

'Cause I know you know you can do it

Peace Lives

Determined to keep peace alive

Accomplished with a sweet prayer

Thankful for what we survived

Continuing to speak real

Or silence is what we decide

Peace should reach it's peak then

No competing, each wins, Peace Friend!

Peace Hopes

Not living in the past helps

Believing is the key

And you should do it 'til your last breath

Hope can be influenced, don't dilute it

Don't take half-steps, have greater faith

Faith that doesn't fade away

Knowing Jesus made a way

Peace Is

Established in our hearts with

The guarantee of sun shines

No thoughts of the dark

Plenty peace is what I'm driven to

It's peace that helps me park

Know peace can be the key

Inciting it's a start

PHILIPPEANS 4:7

And the peace of God which surpasses all understanding will guard your hearts and you minds in Christ Jesus

PROVERBS 30:5-6

Every word of God proves true, he is a shield to those who take refuge in him. Do not add to his words, lest he rebuke you and you be found a liar

The perfect aim, the perfect spot

The perfect shot, the target hit

The quality and quantity

Of the resources you bargain with

It's hard to miss the mark if it's the heart

But not for pain sake

It's for peace sake and the love you feel

The flavor is a sweet taste

Defeat hate, for God is Love

And even when you can't show

Possess the truth, Progress to proof

When people said you can't glow

Relief is already on the road

Receive it and rest

Jesus will save your soul if you believe and confess

Complete to the crest

Abide with the Most High

Where friction is fiction

Without resistance you coast by

The Lord Can

The Lord Will

The Lord Has

Do you believe?

The time is now, His will be done

The wheel is spun

Will you receive?

PSALM 91:1-2

He who dwells in the shelter of the Most High will abide in the shadow of the Almighty. I will say to the LORD, "My refuge and my fortress, my God in whom I trust."

ROMANS 8:31

What then shall we say to these things? If God is for us, who can be against us?

I'm positive impossible is possible

Though unexplained

The angels have a lot to do

We overcame the obstacles

Now unrestrained

Unstoppable

The chains broke

Know God is for us, He adores us

No more vain hope

Help sing the chorus you don't need skill

Thankful that you breathe still

Amazing grace an amazing face

With a smile that's believed real

1 PETER 2:16

Live as people who are free, not using your freedom as a cover up for evil, but living as servants of God

Revelations by inspiration

I wonder what comes of it

By faith shown in demonstrations

Impressions of commonsense

Flow forward toward what you want

Hope nothing could come against it

Maturity magnification

One-on-ones done and defenseless

I'm Thomas, I'm honest

I need to see to believe sometimes

Reasons for grievance so petty

Emotions relieved in a rhyme

Jesus sweet Jesus I need more

Please, give me peace for my mind

Rewrite and reread it

Until I feel I am pleased with designs

Come closer complete this

It is the season to spring

Being the best I can be

Not letting "Less" be a thing

I know what real is

Unquestioned

Line up, be next for some wings

I give expressions not second guesses

So you know just what I mean

Some sights too beautiful to text of

Yeah you know just what I seen

Invision jewels of true love

Crowned on the head of a Queen

It's worth the chance that I take

So fake don't edge in between

I may have limits and timidness

And I fight to be clean

I gave today to know fate

Might as well give night to a dream

I know what's right

But don't know what's left

Or if what's left should be reconvened

PROVERBS 4:18

But the path of the just is like the shining sun, that shines ever brighter unto the perfect day.

Should go the way that makes a way

Not takes away

In place of hate put patience

Not to shine would be a wasted day

Just as justice to the just

Is such as love is to the toughest

You may step heavy, but helped carry

Then honored with abruptness

So suddenly in touch with peace

So much increase, be overwhelmed

A glow that oh so overflows

It never was below the rim

Notice her and notice him

It's hard to miss a star

Though it's farther than you knew

You keep them closer to your heart

Love your neighbor as you love yourself

It shows but not for show

Trust enables, do you trust in depth

Enough that you can grow

As before

Keep shining

To the peak

Keep climbing

Though there's pressure

You can dig it

You will soon reach diamonds

LUKE 18:16

But Jesus called them to him, "Let the children come to me, and do not hinder them, for such belongs to the Kingdom of God.

The smile of a child with a giant heart

I have a hope

That you will grow into a flying star

Maybe the highest, the brightest

Maybe the biggest, the best

Someday your light will be guidance

So share your gift with the next

It's never too early to be great

Like free cake and ice cream

As you live more and you give more

Sky is the limit

As you might dream

Always try hard because you'll fly far

Now it's time to start

You have the right wings

Always be brave

No matter how scary it might seem

How can I begin to commend you

Great job! Well done?

It seems sometimes you shine but don't intend to

I just recommend that you continue true

Don't relent

The only thing that's worse than reversing

Is someone on the fence

Choose sides, the future's wide

But narrow when you're uncertain

Insert heart, love strong

Rest comes when you're done working

Remember you're just one person

One piece to one puzzle

Want completeness

Gather together,

Better

Beyond struggles

New face, a new force

I knew the source

The heart of course

A new day, a new door

A cool core

The heart, of course

Refuse hate, collect respect

Repeat peace

Forgive, Forgive

You lose...wait!

Who loses ?

If I win you win

I live to give

ROMANS12:18

If it is possible, as much as depends on you, live peaceably with all men.

PSALM 85:7

Show us your steadfast love, O LORD, and grant us your salvation

Faith, hope, and love

Grace is mine, peace is felt

Thankyou Father for the victory

In Jesus we prevail

Recede from self, indeed is death

But then true life revealed

I know that alone, hope is gone

But I win by Your Will

I expect the best, the very best

On every test, an A-plus

Not my grades but by your grace

So your glory is made plush

So amazing, no disgrace, I don't worry to race

"Rush"

So emblazed by your spirit

In His story I'm saved

Trust

In His steadfast love, no mask or gloves

Identify

No disguise, love to Infinity

Beyond what you can hide

He arrived and then He died

Then was risen from the grave

He ascended to the Father

Who he's seated with today

Interceding for the people who believe

Depend in faith

Enter ease, His friendship's easy

And never goes away

DEUTERONOMY 31:6

Be strong and courageous. Do not be afraid or terrified because of them, for the LORD your God goes wit you, he will never leave you nor forsake you.

PHILIPPIANS 1:7

It is right for me to feel this way about you all, because I hold you in my heart, for you are all partakers with me of grace, both in my imprisonment and in the defense and confirmation of the Gospel

Commanded but not demanded

Decisions and choices

In lands where I'm never stranded

Divisions of voices

Opinions and common senses

Uniting the forces

For Love and for peace

Jesus

Understand what the source is

Desires to overcome

Come over be soldier too

Be girded with truth, be true

You got it

I know you do

The first and the last

The past, present, and future

We skirt some, we crash sometimes

But never are losers

Experience taught us endurance

We fall then we rise up

Ascended on top of <u>Assurance</u>

What life is inside of

Yeah I knew that having patience

And waiting would pay it's due

I have to admit it hasn't been easy

With reason I've been confused

Thinking I might lose if I don't choose

It could all be lost at anytime

All the construction I've conducted

A lot of them see

But many are blind

Resent or rewind I'd never do

Only one chance is how I see it

That's why I'm direct no need for illusions

I'm loyal to self

Without reasons for treason

So forward I step

I know where to go

No doubt that the destination is decent

Follow the code: Be Bold

I know that you know it

When you're ready begin the sequence

3....2....1.....TAKE OFF!!!!!

Unique thoughts

Speak, talk

Humility says who you are

Your, confident, capable, stable, and true

The place of the prize is not too far

Unique thoughts

You think, Lost

But losing what's useless to gain space

Rearrange grace

Maneuver

You'll never have bitter and sweet in the same taste

Don't settle for waste be Super

The better your attitude: better the future

It's good to be tutored be nobody's fool

Don't stoop to their level

Be cooler!

Unique thoughts

No cheap talk

A priceless device is a kind word

Sometimes we define what love is

To step up and Sheppard a blind herd

Who understands that in a man's hands

Are capable deeds

That in his mind is growing strength

He finds a way to succeed

Who understands that in a woman's eyes

Are beauties unique

She know she does what a man can't

The future repeats

Who understands that in a child's heart is trust

Them believing that, when seeing times get rough

Mom and Dad will be enough

Who understands that when you're elderly

You'll need some help

But still will have the heart

To try providing life and feed yourself

Who understands that there's a plan

One where God is in control

Where there's Love for everyone

A shinning light for heavy souls

Who understands that pain is real

Sometimes you can't contain it's chill

And you shiver, letting tears flow

Rivers of how you feel

But you still grow

And still know

Perseverance is how to build

GOD IS REAL!

1 TIMOTHY 1:5,

The aim of our charge is love that issues from a pure heart and a good conscience and a sincere faith.

PROVERBS 11:25

Whoever brings blessing will be enriched, and one who waters will himself be watered.

PHILIPPIANS 3:4-5

Let your reasonableness be made known to everyone. The lord is at hand do not be anxious about anything, but in everything by prayer and supplication with thanksgiving let your requests be made know to God

I'm not selfish but self defensive

The enemy lurks

I commit my way to my Savior's entrè

And then His desserts

Noah replenished the earth

Jesus has finished His works

Made us a way

Be forgiven for sins

Put an end to the curse

It's not my fault I inherited

The heritage of excuses

I can do it but not used to

The truth of me in His future

An eternal life?

That's hard to grasp

Goggle cannot compute it

Discerning light

Not fire

The Holy Spirit illumined

A lot of this my logic missed

The promise fits if love is true

It ain't hard to get, make it hard to quit

Don't sit, take a standSomeone's love is due

JAMES 1:5

If any of you lacks wisdom, let him ask God, who gives generously to all without reproach and it will be given him

www.ingramcontent.com/pod-product-compliance
Lightning Source LLC
Chambersburg PA
CBHW070114230526
45472CB00004B/1250